GALORE PARK

So you <u>really</u> want to learn

Junior English
Book 2
Answer Book

Andrew Hammond MA

Series Editor: Susan Elkin MA BA (Hons) Cert Ed

www.galorepark.co.uk

Published by Galore Park Publishing Ltd
19/21 Sayers Lane, Tenterden, Kent TN30 6BW
www.galorepark.co.uk

Typesetting by Typetechnique, London
Printed by CPI Antony Rowe, Chippenham and Eastbourne

ISBN-13: 978 1 902984 86 5

First published 2007, reprinted 2008, 2010, 2011

Details of other Galore Park Publications are available at www.galorepark.co.uk

ISEB Revision Guides, publications and examination papers may also be obtained
from Galore Park.

FSC
www.fsc.org
MIX
Paper from
responsible sources
FSC® C013604

Contents

Introduction

The following book offers teachers and parents a range of recommended answers to the questions in *Junior English Book 2*.

In some cases an answer will be a definitive one – regurgitating literal information, writing a definition, or adding a prefix, for example – but there are many other instances when questions require more reflection and as a result, answers will vary. This is good practice, for English at this level is not an exact science. Children need to be encouraged to reflect, consider and express opinions in response to what they have read. For such questions, suggested answers are offered here, but they do not need to be taken too literally, or followed too rigidly. The beauty (and the frustration!) of language learning is that there may be an infinite range of acceptable answers out there. If the children have articulated their views coherently, and supported what they have said with some direct reference to the passage, they must be rewarded.

When working through the questions with your class or child, encourage them to see how the meaning of a word or phrase is always inextricably linked to the context in which it appears – i.e. the sentence that surrounds it. There are many questions that ask for translations, or definitions, of words and phrases. In these cases particularly, it is important to encourage young readers to 'go back to the text' and see how the author has used the word or phrase in the specific context. This is good preparation for Common Entrance, which requires careful, and repeated, reading of passages to ascertain meanings, draw inferences and deductions and reach conclusions. To this end, line references are given throughout *Junior English Book 2*.

Likewise, the old adage, 'read the question carefully' applies, and one might add 'read the answer' too, for mistakes are often missed in the rush to reach the end of a comprehension exercise. Above all, the children need to move beyond a cursory glance at passages and accompanying questions if they are to avoid those tangential answers that can be so costly in examinations.

Comprehension tasks are most effective when they encourage readers to *think* about what they are reading and *communicate* their relevant responses in efficient and enlightening ways. I hope that *Junior English Book 2* and this accompanying answer book, assist you in encouraging children to become thoughtful, confident and communicative students.

Good luck.

A.J.H.
February 2007

Chapter 1

Exercise 1.1

1. Words and phrases may include: night (line 2); dark shadows (line 2); silver glow (line 3); moonlit (line 4).

2. The forest creatures keep warm during the winter by huddling deep in their nests below the frozen ground.

3. From the outside, you can tell that there is someone inside the castle by the light in the window.

4. The queen received a shock when the needle pierced her finger and caused three drops of blood to drip onto the snow-covered window sill.

5. The queen thought of pale skin because of the white snow. The drops of blood caused her to think of rosy red lips and the ebony window frame reminded her of black hair.

6. Answers may vary; suggestions include:
   The references to the 'frozen shroud' and 'ice-latticed tree-tops' give the story a fairytale feeling, though the mention of the 'creaking chill' and the 'cold of the long winter' also creates a sad mood, as we feel sympathy for the frail queen. If the story had been set in summer, the atmosphere, like the weather, may have been warmer and brighter, with references to green fields, blue sky, and so on, though the traditional fairytale feeling may have been lost.

7. Possible definitions are:
   (a) *nook:*   a small, secluded place or corner
   (b) *refuge:*   shelter or place of protection
   (c) *gusted:*   blew forcefully
   (d) *murmured:*   whispered, uttered in a low voice

Exercise 1.2

1. 12% of the Earth's surface is covered in permanent snow or ice.

2. A single snowstorm can drop 40 million tons of snow.

3. The largest snowflake ever recorded measured 38cm across and was 20cm thick.

4. The weather conditions in New York on 3rd November 1958 were surprising because rain was falling on 34th Street whilst guards were making snowballs on top of the Empire State Building.

5. Saudi Arabia has a very hot climate, so it would be surprising to see snow falling in Riyadh.

6.   Possible definitions are:
        (a) *permanent:* lasting, continuing in the same state
        (b) *equivalent:* equal in value, the same as
        (c) *blizzard:* heavy storm of wind and snow
        (d) *website:* location on the Internet consisting of related web pages

Exercise 1.4

1.   The <u>snowflakes</u> fell gently onto the cold <u>stones</u>.
2.   Her <u>eyes</u> filled with <u>tears</u>.
3.   The sharp <u>needle</u> pierced her <u>finger</u>.
4.   About 12% of the <u>surface</u> of the Earth is covered in <u>snow</u> and <u>ice</u>.
5.   The largest <u>snowflake</u> landed in Montana in America.

Exercise 1.5

1.   The queen named her little child Snow White.
2.   The guards made snowballs high up on the Empire State Building.
3.   The snowiest winter in Great Britain was in 1947.
4.   Snow didn't usually fall in Saudi Arabia.
5.   Snow White had skin as pale as white snow.

Exercise 1.6

1.   The postman delivered the letters.
2.   My son ate some apples.
3.   Yesterday Michael took the dog for a walk.
4.   The policeman arrested the thief and took him to the station for questioning.
5.   A wasp stung Gran.

Exercise 1.7

1.   High on a hill above the ice-latticed treetops stood a castle.
2.   Close by the window sat a queen quietly sewing and looking out over the frosty scene.
3.   She gazed thoughtfully at the crimson stains colouring the white snow and her sad eyes filled with tears.
4.   The queen's lips had trembled; 'I will call her Snow White,' she murmured.
5.   The good queen died but her child was, indeed, a daughter.

Exercise 1.8

Masculine	Feminine
prince	princess
actor	actress
uncle	aunt
groom	bride
nephew	niece
lord	lady

Exercise 1.9

1.   host   hostess
2.   teacher   –
3.   lion   lioness
4.   child   –
5.   tiger   tigress
6.   headmaster   headmistress

Chapter 2

Exercise 2.1

1. (a) Stella is Michael's dog.
   (b) her tail circling wildly
2. Michael's boat was called the *Peggy Sue*.
3. A howling from the trees made the hackles on Stella's neck stand up.
4. Michael wanted to climb to the rocky summit of the hill so that he could see further out to sea.
5. Answers may vary; a suggested answer is:
   I think Michael is a very brave boy. Left alone on an island, tired, weak, and haunted by the sound of howling from the trees, he may have been tempted to despair and do nothing, but he decides to press on and find a higher vantage point where he can get his bearings and decide what to do next. He does not give up hope.
6. Possible definitions are:
   (a) *hackles:* hairs that stand on end on the neck and back of an animal, e.g. a dog
   (b) *plaintive:* expressing sorrow, sounding very sad
   (c) *menacing:* looking dangerous or threatening
   (d) *sparsely:* thinly

Exercise 2.2

1. Answers may vary; a suggested answer is:
   The island is described as 'heaven on earth' because of its natural beauty and peaceful atmosphere.
2. Answers may vary; a suggested answer is:
   The cottages have ornate ceilings, built to an impressive design.
3. In the Palm Grove dining pavilion there are sumptuous dishes on offer and a weekly Meke song and dance pageant, which features a traditional Lovo feast.
4. This type of holiday could be recommended to: (a) a family with teenage boys, because of the range of facilities and outdoor pursuits available, and / or (b) a honeymoon couple, for the peace and tranquillity, the romantic location and scenery, and the outdoor pursuits and facilities.
5. Answers will vary. Look for personal responses and references to the island's facilities and location, to support pupils' answers.

6. Possible meanings are:
    (a) *crystalline:*   clear, transparent, like a crystal
    (b) *thatch:*   plant material, such as straw, used to cover a roof
    (c) *sumptuous:*   luxurious, lavish
    (d) *pageant:*   costumed, colourful parade or ceremony

Exercise 2.4

1. I was washed up on a <u>deserted</u> island.
2. I could hear the <u>soft</u> sound of the sea.
3. High above me, the <u>giant</u> trees swayed.
4. The waves lashed against the <u>jagged</u> rocks.
5. The light faded and the <u>cold</u> night drew in.

Exercise 2.6

1. This is paradise! (exclamation)
2. For room service, dial '0'. (command)
3. The scuba diving course commences at 10.00 am. (statement)
4. When would you like breakfast? (question)
5. Keep all belongings with you at all times. (command)

Exercise 2.8

1. dough   (b) no
2. bough   (d) now
3. tough   (a) puff
4. enough   (c) rebuff
5. through   (e) new

Exercise 2.9

1. most   –   cost lost <u>host</u>
2. plough   –   trough <u>bough</u> through
3. now   –   tow <u>cow</u> low
4. grown   –   clown town <u>sown</u>
5. come   –   home <u>some</u> chrome
6. hour   –   tour <u>sour</u> your
7. tomb   –   comb <u>womb</u> bomb
8. weight   –   height <u>eight</u> sleight

Chapter 3

Exercise 3.1

1. You can tell that the creatures were expecting James because Centipede says 'We've been waiting for you'.
2. James is 'frozen with fear' when he first enters the peach because he is faced with all these insects who might eat him up.
3. It would take the centipede so long to take off his boots because he has so many legs and feet.
4. Answers may vary, but may include: proud, confident, arrogant, mischievous, pest.
5. Answers may vary; a possible answer is:
    Gliding gives the impression of a proud, elegant movement; slithering sounds more like movement that is sneaky, slimy and suspicious. So Earthworm would prefer to think of himself as a glider rather than a slitherer.
6. Possible meanings are:
    (a) *famished:* very hungry
    (b) *petrified:* very afraid, paralysed with fear
    (c) *proudly:* with pride, arrogantly
    (d) *slither:* move smoothly like a snake

Exercise 3.2

1. *Myriapods* means 'lots of legs'.
2. Not all centipedes have one hundred legs. Their number of limbs varies from thirty to three hundred and forty-six, depending on the species.
3. Millipedes are more gentle than centipedes because they are slower moving and only eat plant matter; they never hunt other creatures.
4. Millipedes like to live in damp places, such as soil rich in decomposing leaves.
5. Millipedes protect themselves from predators by coiling tightly, keeping their hard exoskeleton exposed.
6. Possible definitions are:
    (a) *arthropods:* animals with jointed limbs and segmented body, e.g. insects
    (b) *species:* kind or class of animal
    (c) *rodents:* small mammals with pointed teeth for gnawing
    (d) *exoskeleton:* a hard, protective covering on the outside of the animal's body

Exercise 3.4

1.   James <u>thought</u> the insects might <u>hurt</u> him.
2.   Centipede <u>grinned</u> proudly.
3.   Everyone <u>roared</u> with laughter.
4.   Centipedes <u>eat</u> soft-bodied insects.
5.   Millipedes <u>live</u> in damp places.

Exercise 3.5

Answers will vary; some suggestions are:
1.   The football player <u>dashed</u> towards the ball.
2.   The dancer <u>glided</u> across the dance floor.
3.   The rain <u>hammered</u> onto the school roof.
4.   'I feel so happy!' James <u>declared</u>.
5.   The little mouse <u>scurried</u> into a corner and hid.

Exercise 3.6

Joseph and his father were spending the day at the fair.

'I don't want to go in!' exclaimed Joseph. 'It's too dark inside.'

'Don't be silly!' said his father. 'It's only pretend. It's not a real ghost train.'

'But I'm frightened,' said his son.

'You'll be fine. Just hold my hand.' said Dad.

They climbed into a carriage and soon disappeared into the darkness.

'Wow!' said Joseph. 'It's amazing!'

'Help!' cried Dad. 'Stop the train. I want to get off.'

'But I thought you said it's only pretend,' said Joseph. 'Who's the Daddy now?'

Exercise 3.7

1. What an amazing picture!
2. We ate our dinner in the garden.
3. I'm not going up there, it's too high! (though with a full stop is acceptable)
4. Sit down at once!
5. Mary will be arriving at ten o'clock.

Exercise 3.9

1. The space crew said that an early launch was impossible.
2. He packed his portable radio in his suitcase.
3. The winning carrot was an incredible size.
4. Passengers are responsible for their own luggage.
5. She had so much prep to do that it was quite unmanageable.
6. The force field around the alien ship was invisible.
7. The centre forward's attempts to score had been absolutely laughable.
8. The doughnut, bursting with jam, looked irresistible.

Chapter 4

Exercise 4.1

1. Five children are exploring the caves together – Jessica, Tim, Fergus, Billy and Dixie.
2. Jessica was worried that the earth that slid about during the night might continue to slide and then trap them all underneath it.
3. As Jessica spoke, the ground they were sat on rippled and flexed and the slope they had slid down reared up and twisted.
4. They left the torch behind, as they ran out of the cavern.
5. Answers may vary; a suggested answer is: 'Their lungs tight with fear' means their hearts were beating fast and they felt breathless because they were so frightened.
6. Possible definitions are:
    (a) *reared:*   rose up
    (b) *ruins:*   remains of something, fragments, decaying pieces
    (c) *cavern:*   deep cave
    (d) *conclusion:*   summing up, judgement

Exercise 4.2

1. The Diplodocus belongs to a group of dinosaurs called *sauropods*.
2. The dinosaur's long neck enabled it to reach up to feed at the tops of the very tall trees and its small head allowed it to browse amongst the vegetation, where few other dinosaurs could reach.
3. If the Diplodocus had been attacked, it would have used its sheer bulk and long, whip-like tail to defend itself.
4. The Diplodocus would have preferred a drier landscape, because its narrow feet would probably have sunk into wet marsh land, under its colossal weight.
5. The long and flexible neck of the Diplodocus resembles the crane's jib; its sturdy body is like the crane's heavy base, preventing it from toppling over.
6. Possible definitions are:
    (a) *pillars:*   upright column, support or structure
    (b) *vegetation:*   plants
    (c) *ambled:*   moved along gently

(d) *habitat:* natural home of an animal or plant

(e) *mire:* waterlogged, muddy ground, swamp

Exercise 4.4

Full version	Contraction	Missing letters
I will	I'll	w, i
I would	I'd	w, o, u, l
I cannot	I can't	n, o
you have	you've	h, a
he has	he's	h, a

Exercise 4.5

1. 'We will get into awful trouble if anything happens to Tim.'
2. 'That is just an excuse,' said Tim.
3. 'You are just frightened like the rest of us.'
4. 'I am going to see what it is,' said Jessica.'
5. 'We are all going with you,' said Billy.
6. 'We have got to get the torch back.'

Exercise 4.6

1. The dinosaur reached high into the trees to find its dinner.
2. 'We had better run! I think it's starting to rain!' said Tim.
3. We don't know whether it's a bone from a Diplodocus or a Mamenchisaurus.
4. The Diplodocus thundered its way down to the lakeside.
5. The dinosaur museum opened its doors to the public at ten o'clock.
6. 'It's five-thirty and we still haven't seen the T-Rex!' said the visitor.

Exercise 4.7

1. damp   damper   dampest
2. new   newer   newest
3. neat   neater   neatest
4. round   rounder   roundest
5. bold   bolder   boldest

Exercise 4.8

cold	colder	coldest
wide	wider	widest
pretty	prettier	prettiest
lovely	lovelier	loveliest
slim	slimmer	slimmest
brave	braver	bravest
close	closer	closest

Chapter 5

Exercise 5.1

1. The children were always keen to visit the railway because the sound of the trains was their only reminder of a previous life in the busy city.
2. The names of the trains were the Green Dragon, the Worm of Wantley and the Fearsome Fly-by-night.
3. The man was a nice looking gentleman with a fresh-coloured, clean-shaven face and white hair. He wore odd-shaped collars and a top-hat that was different to others that the children had seen.
4. The first thing the children noticed about the old gentleman was his hand.
5. The reason given to the children for their father not writing was that he had been 'too busy', but would write soon.
6. The children continued to wave to the old gentleman on the 9.15, in the hope that he might know their father and would meet him. They hoped he would tell Father how his three children stood and waved their love to him every day, from far away.
7. Possible meanings are:
    (a) *omnibuses:*   trad. name for large vehicles/buses taking passengers on set routes
    (b) *tame:*   not wild, domesticated
    (c) *lair:*   animal's den or home
    (d) *custom:*   practice, habit
    (e) *retreat:*   refuge, place to retire or rest

Exercise 5.2

1. (a) The world's first public steam railway was called the Stockton and Darlington line.
    (b) It was 25 miles long.
2. George Stephenson won the Rainhill Trials.
3. The world's first underground passenger railroad opened in London in 1863.
4. For its maiden journey, the Orient Express travelled from Paris in France to Bucharest in Romania.
5. (a) Maglevs are electromagnetic trains.
    (b) Deltics are single-unit diesel-electric locomotives.
6. The New York City Subway opened forty-one years after the London Underground first opened.

7.   Possible meanings are:
    (a) *hauled:*   pulled or dragged with great effort
    (b) *freight:*   commercial transport, cargo
    (c) *investors:*   people who put money into a business venture or enterprise
    (d) *subway:*   underground railway or passage
    (e) *networks:*   interconnecting railways, roads or lines

Exercise 5.4

1.   Mr Halliwell told us that <u>he</u> had been to Jamaica in the holidays.
2.   'Sally, when will <u>you</u> be here?' I asked.
3.   The day trip was fun but <u>it</u> was over too quickly!
4.   Mum gave me a necklace <u>she</u> had bought.
5.   The football players boasted that <u>they</u> would win the game with ease.

Exercise 5.5

1.   Uncle Tom said we should thank <u>him</u> for the weekend.
2.   I wrote to the players to congratulate <u>them</u> on their glorious win.
3.   For Dad's birthday I gave <u>him</u> a gold fountain pen.
4.   When Mum gets home I shall make <u>her</u> a nice cup of tea.
5.   The weather started well but we saw <u>it</u> become worse as the day wore on.

Exercise 5.6

1.   Peter and I went swimming.
2.   Sally and he were friends.
3.   Did you see us yesterday?
4.   They heard you and me laughing.
5.   You and I will go home together.

Exercise 5.7

1.   The children <u>moved</u> to the countryside.
2.   The Green Dragon <u>roared</u> through the countryside.
3.   Peter <u>heard</u> the midnight express <u>go</u> by.

4. The gentleman <u>smiled</u> at the children.
5. Phyllis <u>missed</u> her father very much.

Exercise 5.8

1. <u>Trains</u> replaced <u>horses and oxen</u>.
2. <u>Inventors</u> discovered <u>steam power</u>.
3. <u>The train</u> hauled <u>passenger cars</u>.
4. <u>The company</u> held a <u>competition</u>.
5. <u>Robert Stephenson</u> assisted <u>his father George</u>.

Exercise 5.9

1. <u>Roberta</u> <u>waved and waved</u>.
2. <u>The gentleman</u> <u>smiled</u> back.
3. <u>The Green Dragon</u> <u>trundled</u> on.
4. <u>The London Underground</u> <u>opened</u> in 1863.
5. At last the <u>Channel Tunnel</u> <u>was</u> complete.

Exercise 5.10

1. unhappy
2. pre-ordained
3. semicircle
4. disappoint
5. misinterpret

Exercise 5.11

1. goodness
2. helpful
3. strengthen
4. contentment
5. friendship

Chapter 6

Exercise 6.1

1. The elephant now lives and travels with a circus.
2. Answers will vary; a suggested answer follows:
    By referring to the elephant as 'His Majesty' the poet may be emphasizing his size, stature and the way he is valued and respected by those who come to see him.
3. Answers will vary; a suggested answer follows:
    It is possible that the elephant may not be happy. The poem suggests that there is much he might miss from his natural home in the wild. However, not all of the memories recalled are happy ones – the cry of hungry beasts, the thunder of feet and the dark and dreadful heat – so, perhaps the elephant does not mind being away from these things.
4. 'Chills the spine' might mean that the sound of the wolf's howl causes a spine-tingling fear in the listener.
5. Answers will vary; a suggested answer is:
    By repeating the word 'mine' so many times, the poet encourages us to consider the wolf's point of view, causing us to feel more sympathetic towards it, as it has real feelings and thoughts, just like us.
6. Each stanza offers an alternate, a,b,a,b rhyming scheme, with the slight exception of line 3 in the first stanza.
7. Possible meanings are:
    (a) *dawn:*   first light, daybreak
    (b) *stir:*   to move, wake or exert oneself
    (c) *howl:*   to wail or cry out loud
    (d) *gloom:*   partial darkness

Exercise 6.2

1. The last Short-haired mountain goat died in 2000 when a tree fell on it.
2. Any three from:
    The Iberian lynx; the brown bear; the harbour porpoise; the monk seal; the marsh fritillary butterfly; the corncrake.
3. These species are in danger because of the loss of their natural habitats, through building development, modern farming techniques and climate change.

4.   Answers will vary and may include references to:
      deforestation
      pollution
      building developments
      road-building
      neglect and lack of care
5.   We must look after our soil because it provides us with food to eat, and there is only a tiny proportion of the earth we can use for this.
6.   Possible meanings are:
      (a) *endangered:* at risk, threatened with extinction
      (b) *extinct:*   no longer in existence; died out
      (c) *decline:*   a gradual deterioration
      (d) *habitat:*   an animal's natural enivronment or home

Exercise 6.5

1.   Henry claimed that the winning ticket was his.
2.   The football team believed that victory would soon be theirs.
3.   The Porsche is mine.
4.   Nell took Jane's picture home by mistake and left hers at school.
5.   Is this pencil case yours?

Exercise 6.6

1.   Tilly's rucksack
2.   Mrs Johnson's table
3.   Gran's motorbike
4.   Yoseph's chocolate cake
5.   the children's coats

Exercise 6.7

1.   the chickens' eggs
2.   the men's final
3.   the sheep's pen
4.   the teachers' staff room
5.   the horses' stables

Exercise 6.8

1.   a company of soldiers
2.   a flock of sheep
3.   a gang of thieves
4.   a litter of puppies
5.   a shoal of fish
6.   a quiver of arrows
7.   a plague of locusts
8.   a library of books

Exercise 6.9

1.   a bouquet of flowers
2.   a gaggle of geese
3.   a string of pearls
4.   a fleet of ships
5.   a galaxy of stars
6.   a clutch of eggs
7.   a batch of bread
8.   a colony of ants

Chapter 7

Exercise 7.1

1. Barney began to call the creature 'Stig' because the first sound it made resembled the sound 'Stig'.
2. Answers may vary on the following theme:
   Barney might have thought Stig clever because he fashioned a broken piece of flint into a sharp cutting tool and was able to cut through the creeper that held Barney's legs.
3. Barney liked Stig's home so much because it was packed full of lovely clutter and fascinating objects, which he had not bothered to tidy up.
4. Stig collects water by catching drips from a crack in the roof in a bicycle mudguard. The water runs along the mudguard, through the tube of a vacuum-cleaner and into a large can.
5. Answers will vary. Look for references to Stig's unusual habits and inventive skills, and his cluttered home.
6. Possible definitions are:
   (a) *creepers:*   creeping or climbing plants
   (b) *squatted:*   sat on heels
   (c) *protested:*   strongly objected, declared
   (d) *bracken:*   large ferns
   (e) *niche:*   small hole, gap or recess (e.g. in a wall)

Exercise 7.2

1. Answers may vary; suggestions follow:
   Reduce means to make something smaller in size or amount.
   When we *reuse* something we reclaim it for the same – or a different – purpose.
   To *recycle* means to reprocess something for use again.
2. The writer encourages us to think about how we can reduce packaging when we shop.
3. Answers may vary and may include:
   Shoppers could take their own bags to the shops, instead of receiving yet more plastic bags. We could buy our fruit and vegetables from a local greengrocer who uses low-impact brown bags.
4. Plastic tubs can be used to store things, or as plant pots.
5. Recycling three glass bottles could save enough energy to power a television for over three hours (or three televisions for over one hour).

6.   Possible meanings are:
         (a) *packaging:*   material used for packing
         (b) *cellophane:*   thin, transparent plastic used for wrapping
         (c) *inventive:*   creative, showing original thought
         (d) *annual:*   yearly

Exercise 7.4

1.   'Hullo!' said Barney.
2.   'Oh puff!' said Barney, 'I can't reach my feet. You do it, Stig!'
3.   'My knife!' protested Barney.
4.   'I wish I lived here,' said Barney.
5.   'Golly!' he said. 'You *are* clever! I bet my Grandad couldn't do that, and he's *very* good at making things.'

Exercise 7.5

1.   'I've made a new friend today,' said Barney.
2.   'David! Don't leave your litter on the floor!' cried Mum.
3.   'Have you washed your hands after your adventures?' asked Mum.
4.   'Please do not leave crisp packets on the grass,' said the park attendant.
5.   'Mr Stig, do you like living in this cave?' whispered Barney.

Exercise 7.6

1.   At the end of the road turn right.
2.   Mix the flour and water together to make a paste.
3.   After fitting the drawers, screw the handles onto the front.
4.   In an emergency call 999.
5.   Put all items of litter in the bins provided.
6.   Relax in our luxury Jacuzzi.

Exercise 7.8

1.   eighteen
2.   weight
3.   thief

4.   believe
5.   neighbour
6.   priest

Chapter 8

Exercise 8.1

1. The word *neighbourhoods* helps us to imagine lots of different creatures, all living in the same area. The author has used personification to increase the appeal of the animals, and the ease with which we can picture their 'human-like' homes.
2. The 'crunch' would come if the passing boot stepped on a crab.
3. Repeated use of the letter pattern *cl* accentuates the 'clicking' sound of the crabs.
4. Answers may vary; a suggested answer is:
   The word *sludgy* sounds almost onomatopoeic. It conjures up images of thick, gloopy, wet sand, over which we might trudge slowly.
5. Answers may vary; a suggested answer is:
   The word *dancing* increases the appeal of the crabs, as we picture them moving in a comical, rhythmical or musical way.
6. Possible meanings are:
   (a) *tepid:* quite warm, lukewarm
   (b) *hapless:* unlucky
   (c) *molluscs:* hard-shelled creature with soft body, e.g. snail
   (d) *tango:* South American dance
   (e) *mudflats:* muddy area of beach exposed at low tide

Exercise 8.2

1. Pie-crust crabs earned their name because the top part of their shell resembles the pastry lid of a pie.
2. If you found a pie-crust crab in a rock pool you would know that it was only a young one because the older crabs move down the beach in search of deeper water.
3. The other eggs are probably washed away or eaten by predators.
4. The crab swallows lots of water which causes the old shell to expand and split. The crab then pulls itself backwards out of the old shell.
5. Setae enable the pie-crust crab to feel its way around as it climbs over seaweed and into dark places between rocks.

6.   Possible meanings are:
       (a) *aggressive:*   hostile, threatening
       (b) *scavengers:*   searchers for food
       (c) *crevice:*   tight gap, chink or crack, e.g. in rocks
       (d) *exoskeleton:* a skeleton found on the outside of an animal, e.g. crab

Exercise 8.7

1.   They sat beside the river and ate their picnic.
2.   When they arrived at the beach, Mike and Aziz ran into the sea.
3.   'Don't walk through the woods alone,' said Aunt Jane.
4.   Mary did not like the hot sun, so she found a nice shady spot under a large tree.
5.   Excited about their day trip, the children climbed eagerly onto the coach.

Exercise 8.8

1.   'Is this seat taken?' asked the lady on the bus.
2.   I met a very helpful person in the supermarket.
3.   Julie said she had been bitten by a mosquito.
4.   After a long day in the garden, Grandpa's back was beginning to stiffen.
5.   The Christmas season is nearly upon us.

Exercise 8.9

kitten	skeleton
seven	lemon
bitten	poison
fasten	season
sudden	mutton

Chapter 9

Exercise 9.1

1. Ruth says, 'Where am I?' when she wakes up again, which shows that she does not know her whereabouts.
2. The strangers know that Ruth is Polish because of the Polish names that she cries when she wakes up.
3. Jan boasts that the Ballickis would all have drowned if it had not been for him, and then he gives a dramatic account of the rescue.
4. Answers will vary. Look for references to Ruth's fears that they she may never see her mother again, and her relief when they are reunited at last.
5. Answers will vary. Descriptions may include: caring, loving, brave, patient, understanding, sensitive and fair.
6. Possible meanings are:
    (a) *bewildered:* puzzled, confused
    (b) *smothered:* covered, enveloped
    (c) *mischief:* naughtiness, high jinks
    (d) *eager:* strongly wishing or desiring

Exercise 9.2

1. Anne says that she goes to the attic most mornings to 'clear the stuffy air out of [her] lungs'.
2. Answers will vary; a suggested answer is:
    I think that the 'spell' that Anne is referring to is the atmosphere created by the lovely fresh air and the beautiful views from outside.
3. It was hard for Anne to see the dividing line because the horizon and the sky were the same colour.
4. Anne is cheered up by the 'beauty of nature' that surrounds her and the peace she finds in the attic, where she can be 'quiet' and 'alone with the heavens, nature and God'.
5. Answers will vary and may include references to Anne's courage, patience, eloquence, her love of nature and her strong faith.

6.   Possible definitions are:
   (a) *perked:*   cheered, brightened
   (b) *remedy:*   cure, way of relieving
   (c) *solace:*   consolation, comfort
   (d) *bliss:*   total happiness, heavenly feeling

Exercise 9.5

1.   I slowly realised that I was being watched.
2.   David stared jealously at Harry's new football.
3.   Jane had to run fast to catch up with her friends.
4.   The place was quiet when we arrived here.
5.   When the final exam finished, I danced happily out of the room.

Exercise 9.6

1.   It was dark when Ruth opened her eyes.
2.   'Where am I?' she said.
3.   Ruth reached out her arms to Jan and gave him a hug.
4.   Nearly every morning I go to the attic where Peter works to blow the stuffy air out of my lungs.
5.   But I looked out of the open window too, over a large area of Amsterdam.

Exercise 9.7

Chapter 14

City of the Lost

It was the end of May when the train reached Berlin – after nine days of stopping and starting, of lying up in sidings, of crawling along the battered track.

The station was a shambles, but everyone was glad to escape from the cramped quarters. They swarmed out of the trucks into the dusty ruins of Berlin.

Exercise 9.8

1. It was a special occasion and Mum was baking a cake.
2. This afternoon we completed some comprehension work.
3. I listened carefully to my instructions.
4. We soon realised that we were driving in the wrong direction!
5. Without the right revision, I will be unable to pass the examination.

Exercise 9.9

Suggested definitions are:

1.	*concussion:*	injury caused by blow to the head
2.	*evaporation:*	liquid turned to vapour
3.	*circulation:*	flow of blood from, and back to, the heart
4.	*concession:*	act of conceding, acknowledgement, admission
5.	*suction:*	drawing of air or liquid
6.	*destruction:*	ruin, downfall
7.	*excursion:*	journey, trip
8.	*pension:*	regular payment received after retiring from work
9.	*function:*	purpose, duty / social event
10.	*diversion:*	detour or turning

Chapter 10

Exercise 10.1

1. 'The wind sang through his iron fingers' means that the wind made a whistling, musical sound as it blew through the giant's fingers.
2. This is the first time that the Iron Man has seen the sea.
3. During his fall from the cliff top, the Iron Man broke up into pieces, as his legs, arms, hands, ears, eyes and his head all broke off and went crashing down the rocks onto the beach below.
4. One of the Iron Man's hands ended up lying beside an old, sand-logged washed-up seaman's boot on the beach.
5. Answers will vary.
6. Answers will vary. Look for reasons to support the choices made.
7. Possible meanings are:
   (a) *brink:*   edge, verge
   (b) *infra-red:*   invisible electromagnetic rays
   (c) *snag:*   obstacle or difficulty
   (d) *wheeling:*   moving in a circle or curve

Exercise 10.2

1. It was particularly surprising to see a poster about an Iron Man who 'walks, sits and obeys commands' in the 1930s because this was long before robots, computers, or space travel had been invented.
2. Closed curtains would make the audience feel curious about what lay behind them.
3. (A drawing by the pupil.)
4. The iron man refused to obey the professor's first request to stand because it was only when he used a certain phrase that the iron man would respond, and he had not used it yet.
5. The iron man lifted each of his arms in turn, and bent each knee. Then he walked down a ramp into the audience, turned and then returned to the stage, where he sat down.
6. Answers will vary. Look for good references to the passage and sensible theories.

7.   Possible answers include:
        (a) *emblazoned:*   decorated, displayed
        (b) *demonstration:*   an act of showing something
        (c) *antennae:*   plural of *antenna* – aerial or feeler, e.g. on insect's head
        (d) *interspersing:*   sprinkling, interrupting, supplementing
        (e) *ponderously:*   heavily, clumsily

Exercise 10.6

1.   The tractor drove into the boggy field and got stuck.
2.   We were losing at half-time but we won in the end.
3.   Are you coming with us or are you staying at home?
4.   Carolyn likes spiders but her brother is frightened by them.
5.   James ate all his sweets and then he felt sick.

Exercise 10.7

1.   I set off at eight o'clock because I did not want to be late.
2.   I arrived at the match as the whistle blew for kick off.
3.   I like Spain although I have not been there for years.
4.   We had an awful time in Las Vegas so we never went there again.
5.   Lazy David stared at the television while his mother hoovered around him.

Exercise 10.8

1.   smiling
2.   jumping
3.   living
4.   driving
5.   walking

Exercise 10.9

1.   batting
2.   feeling
3.   shutting
4.   moaning
5.   hitting